BREAKING THE CURSE

BREAKING THE CURSE

Embracing Freedom and Power in Christ

BILL VINCENT

RWG Publishing

CONTENTS

1 Breaking the Curse: Embracing Freedom and Power in Christ   2

2 Part Two   9

3 Part Three   14

About The Author   21

Copyright © 2024 by Bill Vincent

All rights reserved. No part of this book may be reproduced in any manner whatsoever without written permission except in the case of brief quotations embodied in critical articles and reviews.

First Printing, 2024

"I've transformed my sermons into book form. Please note that we've refined the content for clarity and a smoother reading experience. We trust you'll find it engaging."

CHAPTER 1

Breaking the Curse: Embracing Freedom and Power in Christ

I'm sharing this because I genuinely believe it's something we need to hear. This service is likely to be unique, primarily due to the atmosphere we're cultivating. As I was reflecting on the message earlier this morning, my thoughts started to diverge towards various sermon topics. I have a collection of what I call "sermon starters" – ideas I've begun to develop but never fully fleshed out. I must have at least two dozen of these left.

You see, a sermon starter is like a spark that hasn't caught fire. I begin working on it, but for some reason, it never ignites. So, I set them aside, thinking maybe they'll fit into a future message. And this sermon we're about to embark on was initially one of those starters. But as I delved into it, it suddenly clicked. Yes, this is it.

The central theme I want to delve into is "confessions." The title of this message is, "We Are What We Say." Because truly, what we repeatedly speak eventually shapes our reality. It's the fundamental principle at work. Incorrect confessions have the power to ensnare us, while the right ones can liberate us.

We can either find ourselves trapped or set free by our words. If we constantly vocalize weakness, we'll feel weak. Speak of illness, and illness may find a home within us. Discuss poverty incessantly, and we may find ourselves impoverished. Our confessions serve as seeds, fostering the growth of whatever we're verbalizing.

It's crucial to grasp this concept because, within our community, I've noticed instances where individuals inadvertently speak negative outcomes into existence. You know those moments when someone casually says, "I'm losing my mind" or "I feel like I'm going blind"? It's essential to combat those declarations with the power of prayer. Even from a young age, the words we speak can influence our circumstances, potentially binding us.

Regardless of external circumstances, regardless of appearances, we all require a form of confession therapy. For instance, it's tempting to tell our children, "We can't afford it" rather than a straightforward "no." But such statements only reinforce limitations instead of teaching the value of boundaries.

Consider the topic of aging. The more we focus on it, the more we inadvertently accelerate its onset. I've been in ministry for 25 years now, and although I used to be labeled the "young minister," that description has gradually faded. But I refuse to let my age dictate my vitality. Our confessions wield incredible power, akin to exercise for the soul.

Allow me to digress for a moment. Just as physical activity sustains our bodies, so too do positive confessions sustain our spirits. If our bodies are beginning to show signs of wear and tear, the best remedy is movement. Retirement often leads to a sedentary lifestyle, but it's those who remain active that truly thrive. Age becomes irrelevant when we prioritize our well-being.

It's not about undertaking rigorous workouts daily; rather, it's about adopting a lifestyle that promotes health and freedom. Not everyone needs to power walk; sometimes, a leisurely stroll suffices. The key is to get moving and to reframe our confessions to align with a healthier mindset. We must break free from old habits that no longer serve us, as they only perpetuate stagnation.

I look around our neighborhood and see many individuals who've resigned themselves to a sedentary existence. They've become accustomed to inactivity, which inevitably leads to physical decline. My message to them, and to all of us, is simple: Keep moving. Activity breathes life into our bodies, invigorating us both physically and spiritually.

I recall a story about my mother, who at 75, is eligible for a new mobility scooter from the government. While there's nothing inherently wrong with accepting assistance, it's concerning when individuals in their prime start planning for a future of dependency. My brother, in his fifties, already anticipates needing my mother's old scooter someday. But why resign oneself to a fate of limited mobility when there's still so much life to be lived?

I understand that circumstances vary, and sometimes physical limitations are unavoidable. However, I've personally experienced the transformative power of positive confessions and unwavering faith. When I faced physical challenges, I refused to succumb to despair, steadfastly believing in God's promise of healing. And through the combination of prayer and perseverance, I witnessed miracles unfold.

Age is just a number, and how we perceive ourselves profoundly impacts our well-being. Let's reject the notion of premature aging and embrace a mindset of vitality. Instead of succumbing to fatigue, let's cultivate resilience and embrace a lifestyle that fosters health and longevity.

We all have the power to shape our reality through our words and actions. Let's choose to speak life into our circumstances, affirming our potential and embracing a future filled with vitality and purpose.

Why? Because that's your confession. You're anticipating it. One of the most disheartening moments in the doctor's office is when you walk in and they start listing off all the health issues your family members have had. "Your mother had diabetes, your dad had cancer..." It's as if they're prepping you for a future riddled with ailments. But whenever they ask me, "Is there any history of diabetes in your family?" I respond with a resolute "No." My allegiance lies with a different kingdom, one where disease has no place. I once told my doctor "There's no high blood pressure in my father's house."

Sometimes, we need to remind ourselves that dwelling on aging only hastens its arrival. I've heard people in stores exclaim, "I'm getting old," echoing the sentiment of characters like Sanford from the old sitcom "Sanford and Son." Despite his robustness, Sanford would often talk as if he were on death's doorstep. His constant lamentations about arthritis and heart attacks seemed like a self-fulfilling prophecy. It's almost comical, reminiscent of a poorly scripted TV show.

Consider the confessions that emanate from your own household. Positive confessions refuse to yield to physical sensations. It's akin to when my coach used to tell me to "walk it off." At the time, I thought he was nuts, but our bodies are remarkably resilient. We can overcome a lot more than we give ourselves credit for.

Right confessions ignore the signals of pain and discomfort, choosing instead to believe in God's promises. Some folks are quick to diagnose themselves with cancer at the slightest anomaly. I knew a guy who thought he had cancer because of a spot on his neck, only to discover it was a stray cornflake. Our confessions often reflect our expectations. If we constantly anticipate the worst, we shouldn't be surprised when it materializes.

If your ancestors were plagued by various illnesses, it doesn't mean you're destined for the same fate. I refuse to inherit ailments from a lineage I'm no longer bound to. Christianity, in its essence, is a confession. It's a declaration of faith that separates us from the ways of the world.

Hebrews speaks of holding fast to our confession. We're instructed to confess our sins, a practice that reaffirms our salvation. Unlike the rituals of some religious traditions, our confession isn't confined to a confessional booth. It's a direct communication with Jesus, the source of our redemption.

Confession isn't just reciting scripture; it's believing in its truth. Whether it's claiming healing or declaring victory over sin, our words carry power. They shape our reality and ward off the enemy's schemes. So, instead of speaking negativity into existence, let's embrace the liberating truth of God's Word.

There's a tendency, when you discover an unusual ability your body possesses, to showcase it like a circus act. Take, for instance, being double-jointed. People often revel in demonstrating their flexibility, contorting their limbs into peculiar shapes. But by doing so, you inadvertently highlight your joint weaknesses.

I recall a time when I could almost rotate my foot halfway around. Why? Because the ligaments were no longer properly connected. I could twist and turn my ankle at will. But then, God intervened and instructed me to cease. It's never a good sign when God has to intervene in such matters.

Yet, it's challenging to resist showcasing newfound talents. It's like suppressing an itch you can't scratch. Everyone's popping and contorting, reveling in their physical peculiarities. But let's not forget, it's the confession of our mouths that plays a pivotal role in our salvation.

Without a steadfast confession, not only do we risk losing our healing, but we jeopardize our very salvation. The enemy seeks to exploit our weaknesses, driving us to surrender. Many succumb to despair, paving the way for the spirit of death to gain a foothold.

Do you want to give up? Some of you, though young, already feel worn down. But it's time to reclaim your vitality. We're not meant to live in a perpetual state of lethargy. Even kids today spend too much time lounging about, propping their feet up as if it's second nature.

Our bodies aren't designed for prolonged periods of inactivity. We're creatures meant to be in motion, not idle. Yet, our culture often glorifies laziness, normalizing a sedentary lifestyle. But there's a stark difference between someone who's active and someone who's sedentary.

We shouldn't be winded from the simplest tasks, like peeling an orange. It's time for a paradigm shift in our confessions. Yes, it may seem uncomfortable at first, but our words hold the power to shape our reality, for better or for worse.

Consider the impact of your words. Are they affirming life or reinforcing negativity? Whether it's battling addiction or illness, our confessions shape our destiny. Let's break free from the cycle of self-defeating declarations and embrace the liberating truth of God's Word.

Remember, the power of confession isn't limited to spiritual matters. It extends to every facet of our lives. So, let's guard our mouths and speak life into existence. And you have a choice: you can either accept that injury or reject it.

But there are instances where your body's response will be to receive healing. You'll be healed, you'll be whole, because that's how God made you. I remember teaching many years ago about the intricacies of the human body, how blood courses through our veins, the workings of the heart—it's beyond comprehension. Science can't replicate it. God designed our bodies to function. We need to prioritize our health.

I don't know about you, but I'm eager to witness the incredible things God has promised me on this earth. Watching a little baby grow up and become who she's meant to be—I can only imagine the personality she'll have in twenty years. I'm not fixating on where I'll be in twenty years, but I am committed to ensuring my body responds.

I have much yet to see and do, and it's far from over. So, are you ready to change your confessions? Change the way you speak? Stop saying, "I'm broke, I can't afford it"? Stop confessing lack. Because when you speak lack, you give the enemy access.

Our confessions can open doors for the enemy. Are you willing to close those doors? Do you receive this? Lord, we ask that you transform our thinking and empower us to speak truth according to your Word.

Let's start confessing healing, abundance, and blessings. Let's find our confession in the Word of God and use it as our tool and our power. It's time to make a change.

CHAPTER 2

Part Two

Let's dive right into it. We're delving deep. Mark chapter 11, verse 23, tells us, "For verily I say unto you that whosoever shall say unto this mountain, Be thou removed, and be thou cast into the sea, shall not doubt in his heart, but shall believe that those things which he saith shall come to pass, he shall have whatsoever he saith."

It's a potent scripture, straightforward yet profound. But in my recent reflections on faith, I've come to realize there's more to it than meets the eye. The faith movement may have overlooked some aspects that we need to grasp. I'm here to unveil insights that could potentially revolutionize your approach.

We all understand that some methods yield results while others fall short. When something isn't working, it's time for a change. The scripture empowers us, urging us to speak with conviction and authority.

It's crucial to note that the scripture doesn't emphasize prayer alone but the power of words. While prayer is vital, there's a distinct efficacy in declaring with unwavering belief. Let's move beyond mere prayers to declarations that resonate with our connection to the divine.

Words are instrumental in creation; the world itself was spoken into existence. The book of Genesis echoes this truth repeatedly. God's word upholds everything, not prayers but His Word. Every miracle performed by Jesus stemmed from His spoken word.

Let's explore further. Jesus commanded, not prayed, for miracles to happen. Whether it was healing the sick, raising the dead, or calming storms, His words held authority. We're called to emulate this authority, realizing the power vested in us.

Indeed, scripture emphasizes the potency of our declarations. We're not mere observers but active participants in shaping our reality. Let's embrace this truth and step into our identity as agents of change.

Absolutely, I believe it. Paul, Elijah, Joshua, Jesus, they all exemplified the authority of their words. They didn't rely on intermediary phrases like "God said"; their words carried the divine authority because they were in tune with God's will.

These individuals walked in a profound understanding of their identity as children of God, empowered to speak with authority. They didn't hesitate to command the elements or declare divine decrees because they understood their position as vessels of God's power.

Their faith wasn't just theoretical; it was practical and manifested in their words and actions. They didn't need elaborate prayers or rituals; they simply spoke, and things happened.

Their example challenges us to reconsider our approach to faith. Instead of relying solely on prayers, we should boldly declare God's promises and exercise the authority He has given us.

As for the future of the Church, I agree that there's a transformation on the horizon. A new wave of believers will rise, embodying the same authority and boldness as those we read about in the Scriptures.

This faith movement won't be confined to a few charismatic leaders; it will be a grassroots movement of believers who understand their identity and walk in the power of God's Word. They will speak life, healing, and transformation into every situation they encounter.

It's time for the Church to embrace its true identity as agents of change and carriers of God's authority. As we step into this new era of faith, let's remember to always give glory to God for the miracles and transformations we witness.

This story is a powerful reminder of how God works in unexpected ways and through unexpected people. The maintenance man, unaware of the revival happening around him, simply spoke a word of faith to a woman in need, and she received her miracle.

It's heartbreaking to hear how the church responded to this miraculous healing. Instead of rejoicing and embracing the power of God at work, they rejected the man who had spoken the word of faith and ultimately drove him away. The consequences were dire for the woman who lost her healing and returned to her wheelchair.

This story highlights the danger of religious traditions and man-made rules that hinder the free flow of God's power. When we box God into our preconceived notions of how He should work, we limit His ability to move in our midst.

But God is not confined by our human limitations. He can use anyone, anywhere, at any time to accomplish His purposes. All He requires is a willing heart and a faith-filled declaration.

The examples of faith throughout history, from David facing Goliath to Daniel interpreting dreams, remind us that God honors boldness and confidence in His promises. When we speak His word with faith and authority, mountains move, giants fall, and miracles happen.

Religion may question and doubt, but true faith trusts in the power of God's word. It's time for the church to break free from religious constraints and step into the fullness of God's power and authority. Like Smith Wigglesworth, we must boldly declare, "Be healed," knowing that God is always faithful to fulfill His word.

He indeed said, "Be healed," but the circumstances of his ministry were far from conventional. He was a plumber by day and a miracle worker by night. Can you imagine it? There were even photos of him, his hands stained with grease from his daytime work, now out praying for people. Just an ordinary man who believed, truly believed.

Now, I want to leave you with this conclusion, so listen closely. That's how God operated in the past, and He hasn't changed His methods. He's still seeking people through whom He can speak. Will you be that person?

You see, when you conclude, you close the door. But when you speak, it's an open invitation. So, imagine the frenzy in America over someone being crowned. All the pageants, the cheers, the glitz. But in this new wave of glory, power, and authority, as we speak God's word, there will be a level of recognition from the church itself that we've never experienced before.

I've witnessed it myself. People clamoring for a touch, for a word, and we have to direct them to God. No matter the authority we walk in, we must always give Him the glory. Moses exemplified this beautifully. Despite his incredible authority, he always pointed to God, never taking credit for himself.

What I'm seeing by the Spirit, if we grasp it as God intends, it will revolutionize Illinois like never before. So, how will we respond? We must protect His glory, but also be willing to go as deep and as far as He leads us.

Every wheelchair in a hospital will one day be empty in a service. Just look at the examples like William Branham. He didn't even pray sometimes, just spoke with authority. What's your word going to be? God already gave you the instruction: "Be healed."

Are you praying or are you saying? Believe in your words. Keep saying it until you believe it. And when you do, you'll see the change. It's time for you to speak to your circumstances, to your body, to your finances, to your children.

We must believe what we say. And if you're not ready yet, practice with something small. Step out in faith. God is taking us all out of our comfort zones, but it's for a purpose. Get ready, because things are about to get busy. A true revival is on the horizon. Let's praise the Lord!

CHAPTER 3

Part Three

As I was spending some time with the Lord, a profound message dropped into my spirit in a very unexpected manner. It all began when I reflected on a particular experience in my life that compelled me to start writing about it. Interestingly, I had never documented this experience in any of my writings or preached about it before.

The title of this message is quite simple, and I'll delve into it later. At one point in my journey with God and ministry, I encountered a breakthrough where a curse I wasn't even aware of was broken. Have you ever found yourself living a Christian life under a hidden curse? Sometimes we face challenges without understanding their origins.

I wasn't in a religious mindset at the time, unaware that I was operating under a curse. It wasn't necessarily the result of someone practicing magic or sorcery, as depicted in movies, but rather a subtle influence of negative words and energies spoken over my life.

The concept that life and death are in the power of the tongue hit me profoundly. It's not just about God responding to our words, but also about recognizing when we might be living under a curse due to the words spoken over us by others.

Have you ever felt the weight of someone else's words affecting your life? We have the power to speak life or death, blessings or curses, into existence. I've witnessed people seemingly healthy receive a negative diagnosis, only to succumb to it shortly after.

Scripture tells us that we can be satisfied by the fruit of our lips, whether good or bad. When we speak life, blessing, and healing, we set powerful spiritual forces in motion. Even in the midst of challenges, acknowledging God's work and speaking positive affirmations can shift our perspective.

Sometimes, blessings come with financial challenges, but even in those moments, I've learned to trust in God's provision. And while it may seem like we're under a curse, whether from others or self-imposed, we have the authority to break free from it.

Consider the impact of negative words spoken over you, whether by family, colleagues, or even yourself. Words carry power, and when we speak gossip, criticism, or judgment, we empower those words to manifest.

In our society, gossip and negativity have become rampant, even among children. It's essential to recognize the spiritual implications of our words and strive to speak life and positivity instead.

While some may believe that curses are a thing of the past, the reality is that words spoken against us can still hold power. We're called to rise up and condemn every tongue that rises against us in judgment, not to curse back but to break the power of negative words over our lives.

Remember, we're not condemning the individuals but the negative words and energies they speak. Our response to negativity shouldn't be to retaliate with more negativity but to stand firm in the power of positive speech and affirmations.

In essence, life and death truly reside in the power of the tongue.

Until we truly grasp this truth, how many of us have heard this sermon preached? How many have read about it in books?

Yet, despite this exposure, many still lack a deep understanding of its implications. Sisters can even harbor negative thoughts against each other. Words hold immense power in the spiritual realm, just as thoughts do. A fleeting thought can transform into something malevolent in the spiritual realm. If a mere thought can turn dark, imagine the impact of spoken words.

It's a sobering reality that words spoken in gossip and slander can give life to destructive forces. Unfortunately, the stereotype that women are the primary gossipers is debunked when we witness men engaging in similar behavior. I've witnessed men's gatherings devolve into gossip sessions about trivial matters, including remarks about other men's wives. It's a stark reminder of the power of words to fuel negativity and division.

Scripture advises us to take every thought captive because sin often begins in the mind. Thoughts are like the tongue of the mind, capable of steering us toward righteousness or leading us astray. We must guard against negative thought patterns that can spiral into sinful behavior. Our minds are a battlefield, and our thoughts wield significant influence.

I recall a pivotal moment when a renowned prophet visited my church unexpectedly. He revealed that a curse had been hindering my ministry, unbeknownst to me. This curse stemmed from public scrutiny and personal attacks, causing false accusations to tarnish my reputation repeatedly. Despite my confusion, his words resonated deeply, prompting me to confront the reality of spiritual warfare.

The prophet's declaration ignited a sense of urgency within me. I realized that despite my faith and dedication to God, unseen forces were impeding my progress. It was a humbling realization that even as a Christian, I was not immune to spiritual attacks. However, armed with this newfound awareness, I resolved to break free from the grip of the curse.

I uttered a simple prayer, invoking the power of Christ's redemption over my life. Despite my initial skepticism, I embraced the prophet's words with fervent belief. I declared my freedom from the curse, trusting in God's promises of deliverance. It was a transformative moment, marking the beginning of a journey toward spiritual renewal and empowerment.

In retrospect, I recognize the importance of acknowledging the reality of spiritual warfare. As Christians, we are engaged in a constant battle against unseen forces seeking to hinder our progress. However, we possess the authority to overcome every obstacle through Christ who strengthens us. By aligning our words and thoughts with God's truth, we can break free from the grip of curses and walk in victory.

The moment the prophet prayed, it was as if a switch had been flipped. The heaviness that had weighed down the church lifted, making room for a flood of blessings. It wasn't just a spiritual breakthrough; it was a tangible shift in every aspect of our ministry. Finances, anointing, healing—everything surged forward with unprecedented momentum.

I remember that morning vividly. The power of God surged through the room, causing nearly the entire congregation to be overcome by His presence. For me, it felt like a heavy burden had been lifted off my shoulders—a spiritual oppression I hadn't even realized was there until it was gone.

As the prophet left without fanfare, his simple act of obedience had set off a chain reaction of miracles. People were healed, delivered, and set free. The atmosphere crackled with expectancy as God's presence saturated the room.

Our church, once struggling to make ends meet, experienced a radical transformation. What was once a meager offering of $400 a month blossomed into a weekly abundance of $3,000. It wasn't just about the money; it was about the overflow of God's blessings pouring into every area of our lives.

And it wasn't just financial blessings; it was supernatural manifestations like diamonds appearing on the church roof—a tangible reminder of God's favor and provision. It was a season of abundance, where God's goodness overflowed in ways we couldn't have imagined.

But perhaps the most profound change was the internal transformation within our congregation. People who had been bound by sickness, poverty, and spiritual oppression found freedom and breakthrough. Marriages were restored, bodies were healed, and lives were transformed.

It was a powerful testimony to the reality of spiritual warfare and the victory we have in Christ. As we broke free from the curse that had held us captive, we stepped into a new level of spiritual authority and abundance.

Today, I stand as a witness to the transformative power of breaking curses. I've seen it in my own life and in the lives of countless others. And as I speak these words, I believe that chains are being broken, curses are being lifted, and breakthrough is on the horizon for those who dare to believe.

As the words flowed from your lips, it was evident that you were on a mission to break every chain, every curse that dared to hold God's people back. And indeed, I've witnessed the power of breaking curses firsthand.

It's like watching barrenness turn into fruitfulness before your very eyes—a miraculous transformation that only God can orchestrate. And you're right to declare boldly that nothing is impossible for our God!

Your passion to see curses broken, not just in individuals, but over churches, ministries, and even resources, is contagious. You're tapping into a truth that many overlook—that we serve a God who delights in setting His people free from every form of bondage.

And it's not just about physical ailments or genetic predispositions. It's about recognizing the spiritual reality behind every curse, whether it's sickness, poverty, or death itself. These are not God's will for His people, and you refuse to accept them as such.

I couldn't help but smile at your determination to break the cycle of generational curses, to stand firm in your identity as a child of heaven's kingdom. It's a bold declaration of faith, one that refuses to bow to the limitations of the world's expectations.

And your stories—of tumors shrinking, of gray hair turning dark—it's a testament to the power of God's word spoken in faith. You're not just preaching theory; you're sharing real-life testimonies of God's faithfulness and His desire to see His people walk in freedom.

As you declare breakthrough, of curses being shattered and healing flowing like a mighty river, I join you in faith, believing that what God has promised, He is faithful to fulfill. This is a curse-free zone, where chains are broken, and lives are forever changed by the power of His love.

Your words carry the weight of authority, echoing through the room with a determination to see every curse shattered, every chain broken. It's a call to freedom, a call to step into the fullness of God's promises.

As the music swells and hearts are stirred in worship, there's a sense of anticipation in the air—a readiness to confront whatever may have held us back, to lay it all down at the feet of Jesus.

And as you invite each person to come forward, it's like stepping into a sacred moment, a holy exchange where burdens are lifted and chains are cast aside. With a simple wave of your hand and the declaration, "I break the curse," there's a tangible shift in the atmosphere, a release of God's power to set the captives free.

Just as you experienced the power of breaking curses firsthand, its divine intervention, where lives will be forever changed by the touch of God's hand. And as we stand in His presence, we declare with boldness and faith, "Your kind of glory, come down!"

About the Author

Diving deep into the realms of spiritual awakening, Bill Vincent embodies a connection with the Supernatural that spans over three decades. With a robust prophetic anointing, he has dedicated his life to ministry, serving as a guiding light and a pillar of strength in Revival Waves of Glory Ministries.

Bill Vincent is not just a Minister but a prolific Author, contributing to the spiritual enlightenment of many through his diverse range of writings and teachings. His work encompasses themes of deliverance, fostering the presence of God, and shaping Apostolic, cutting-edge Church structure. His insights are drawn from a wellspring of experience, steeped in Revival, and fine-tuned by a profound Spiritual Sensitivity.

In his relentless pursuit of God's Presence and his commitment to sustaining Revival, Bill focuses primarily on inviting divine encounters and maintaining a spiritual atmosphere ripe for transformation. His extensive library of over 125 books serves as a beacon of hope, guiding countless individuals in overcoming the shackles of Satan and embracing the light of God.

Revival Waves of Glory Ministries is not your typical church – it's a prophetic ministry, a sanctuary where the Holy Spirit is given the freedom to move as He wills. Our sermons, a blend of divine wisdom and revelation, can be experienced on Rumble, immersing you in the transformative power of the Word: https://rumble.com/c/revivalwavesofgloryministriesbillvincent

For a deeper exploration into our teachings, visions, and the manifold grace of God, visit https://www.revivalwavesofgloryministries.com/.

Embark on a journey of spiritual discovery with Bill Vincent, and let the waves of revival wash over you, unveiling the divine power and boundless love of God!

Podcast: https://podcasters.spotify.com/pod/show/bill-vincent2

Rumble: https://rumble.com/c/revivalwavesofgloryministries-billvincent

Be sure to check out our new videos **Downloads From Heaven!**

Donate: https://www.revivalwavesofgloryministries.com/giving

Bookstore: https://www.revivalwavesofgloryministries.com/online-stores

Invite Bill Vincent (PREACH, TEACH AND PROPHETIC MINISTRY) to your Event: rwgministry@yahoo.com